DREAM SWITZERLAND: A TRAVEL PREPARATION GUIDE

DANIEL HUNTER

All rights reserved. No part of this publication may be reproduced, distributed, or transmitted in any form or by any means, including photocopying, recording, or other electronic or mechanical methods, without the prior written permission of the publisher, except in the case of brief quotations embodied in critical reviews and certain other noncommercial uses permitted by copyright law.

Copyright © (DANIEL HUNTER) (2023).

TABLE OF CONTENT

CHAPTER ONE
THE SWITZERLAND EXPERIENCE
*WHAT TO EAT AND DRINK IN SWITZERLAND
*WHAT TO BUY IN SWITZERLAND
*BEST MUSEUMS IN SWITZERLAND
*BEST CHURCHES IN SWITZERLAND
*BEST PARKS AND GARDENS IN SWITZERLAND
*ART GALLERIES IN SWITZERLAND

CHAPTER TWO
TRAVEL SMART
*THINGS TO KNOW BEFORE VISITING SWITZERLAND
*GETTING HERE AND AROUND IN SWITZERLAND
*ESSENTIALS
*WHAT TO WEAR FOR EVERY SEASON IN SWITZERLAND
*HELPFUL SWISS PHRASES
*GREAT ITINERARIES

CHAPTER THREE
ACCOMMODATIONS
*BEST PLACE TO EAT, SLEEP AND RELAX
*ENTERTAINMENT AND NIGHTLIFE

CHAPTER FOUR
FUN FACTS ABOUT SWITZERLAND

CHAPTER ONE

THE SWITZERLAND EXPERIENCE
Switzerland is a small country located in the heart of Europe, known for its picturesque mountains, delicious chocolate, and renowned banking system. The Swiss experience is one of natural beauty, cultural diversity, and a high standard of living.

One of the most popular activities in Switzerland is hiking in the Swiss Alps. The mountains offer breathtaking views and a variety of trails for all skill levels. Whether you're a seasoned hiker or a beginner, you'll find a trail that's perfect for you. The Matterhorn, located on the border of Switzerland and Italy, is one of the most famous peaks in the Alps and a popular destination for hikers.

Switzerland is also home to several famous ski resorts, such as Zermatt and St. Moritz. These resorts offer excellent skiing and snowboarding opportunities, as well as other winter activities like ice skating and cross-country skiing. The Swiss Alps are also a popular destination for winter sports enthusiasts.

Switzerland is also known for its delicious chocolate and cheese. Many chocolate and cheese factories offer tours, allowing visitors to learn about the production process and sample the products. Switzerland is also famous for its watches and jewelry, and visitors can find a wide variety of luxury watches and jewelry in Swiss cities such as Geneva and Zurich.

Switzerland has a rich cultural heritage, with four official languages (German, French, Italian, and Romansh) and a diverse population. The country has a long history of neutrality and has played a significant role in international politics. Switzerland is also home to several famous cultural institutions, such as the Jungfraujoch, the highest railway station in Europe, and the Rhine Falls, the largest waterfall in Europe.

Switzerland is also known for its banking system, which is considered to be one of the most stable and secure in the world. Visitors can take advantage of the country's banking services, including opening a Swiss bank account. Switzerland is also home to several international organizations, such as the Red Cross and the World Health Organization, which have their headquarters in Geneva.

Overall, Switzerland offers a unique and unparalleled experience that cannot be found anywhere else in the world. The country's natural beauty, delicious food, rich culture, and stable banking system make it a popular destination for tourists from all over the world.

WHAT TO EAT AND DRINK IN SWITZERLAND

Switzerland is a country known for its delicious food and drink, and there are a variety of traditional dishes and drinks that visitors should try when they visit.

One of the most famous Swiss dishes is Raclette, a traditional cheese dish that is typically served in the winter months. Raclette is made by heating a large wheel of cheese and scraping the melted cheese onto a plate, which is then served with boiled potatoes, pickles, and onions. Another popular cheese dish is Fondue, which is a melted cheese dish that is typically served with bread.

Another traditional Swiss dish is Rösti, a type of potato pancake that is usually served as a side dish. Rösti can be made with grated potatoes, onions, and bacon, and is often served with dishes such as Raclette or Fondue.

Switzerland is also known for its delicious chocolate, and visitors can find a wide variety of chocolate shops and chocolate factories throughout the country. Switzerland is famous for its milk chocolate, which is made with milk from Swiss cows and is considered to be some of the best in the world. Visitors can also find a wide variety of chocolate truffles, chocolate bars, and other chocolate treats in Switzerland.

Switzerland is also known for its wine, particularly its white wines. Swiss white wines are typically made from the Chasselas grape, and are known for their crisp, fruity flavor. Switzerland is also known for its beer, particularly its lagers and pilsners. Swiss beer is typically made with high-quality ingredients and is known for its smooth, refreshing taste.

When it comes to drinks, Switzerland is also known for its coffee culture. Visitors can find a wide variety of coffee shops and cafes throughout the country, serving different types of coffee, including cappuccinos, lattes, and espressos.

Switzerland is also known for its unique and delicious spirits. One of the most famous is Absinthe, which is a green spirit made from wormwood, anise, and fennel. It is traditionally served with a sugar cube and a small amount of water, which is added to the spirit to release the flavors. Another popular spirit is Kirsch, a clear brandy made from cherries. It is often used in cocktails or as a digestif after a meal.

When it comes to eating out, Switzerland has a wide variety of restaurants to choose from, serving everything from traditional Swiss dishes to international cuisine. Some of the most popular restaurants are located in cities such as Zurich, Geneva, and Bern, but visitors can also find great restaurants in smaller towns and villages throughout the country.

In conclusion, Switzerland offers a wide variety of delicious food and drink to visitors, from traditional Swiss dishes such as Raclette and Fondue to delicious chocolate, wine, and beer. Visitors can also find a wide variety of coffee shops and cafes throughout the country, as well as unique and delicious spirits like Absinthe and Kirsch. Whether you're looking for a traditional Swiss meal or an international dining experience, Switzerland has something for everyone.

WHAT TO BUY IN SWITZERLAND
Switzerland is a country known for its luxury goods and high-quality products, and there are a variety of items that visitors should consider buying when they visit.

One of the most famous Swiss products is Swiss watches. Switzerland is known for its watchmaking tradition and is home to some of the world's most famous watch brands such as Patek Philippe, Rolex, and Omega. These watches are known for their precision, craftsmanship, and luxury design. Visitors can find a wide variety of Swiss watches in cities such as Geneva, Zurich, and Basel, as well as in smaller towns and villages throughout the country.

Another popular item to buy in Switzerland is Swiss chocolate. Switzerland is known for its delicious chocolate, which is made with high-quality ingredients and is considered to be some of the best in the world. Visitors can find a wide variety of chocolate shops and chocolate factories throughout the country, where they can purchase chocolate bars, truffles, and other chocolate treats. Swiss chocolate is also a popular souvenir to bring back home.

Switzerland is known for its luxury fashion and clothing. Visitors can find a wide variety of high-end designer stores in cities such as Zurich, Geneva, and Bern, as well as in smaller towns and villages throughout the country. Brands such as Gucci, Prada, and Louis Vuitton have their own shops in Switzerland, offering a wide range of clothing, accessories and footwear.

Switzerland is known for its luxury jewelry, particularly its diamonds. Visitors can find a wide variety of jewelers in cities such as Geneva, Zurich, and Basel, where they can purchase high-end jewelry such as diamond rings, earrings, and necklaces.

Switzerland is known for its luxury home goods, such as tableware and home decor. Visitors can find a wide variety of high-end stores throughout the country, where they can purchase items such as vases, tablecloths, and other home decor items.

Switzerland is known for its fine art and antiques. Visitors can find a wide variety of art galleries and antique shops in cities such as Zurich, Geneva, and Bern, where they can purchase art and antiques from local and international artists and artisans.

Switzerland is also known for its luxury watches, knives, and other small goods. Visitors can find a wide variety of high-end stores throughout the country, where they can purchase items such as pocket watches, Swiss Army knives, and other small luxury goods.

In conclusion, Switzerland offers a wide variety of high-quality and luxury products to visitors, from Swiss watches and chocolate to luxury fashion and jewelry. Visitors can find a wide variety of high-end stores in cities such as Zurich, Geneva, and Bern, as well as in smaller towns and villages throughout the country. Whether you're looking for a high-end watch, a box of delicious chocolate, or a piece of luxury fashion, Switzerland has something for everyone.

BEST MUSEUMS IN SWITZERLAND
Some of the best museums in Switzerland include:

•The Swiss National Museum in Zurich, which has a wide collection of cultural and historical artifacts from Switzerland's past.

•The Museum Rietberg in Zurich, which has a collection of art and artifacts from non-European cultures.

•The Château de Prangins in Nyon, which is a 18th-century castle that houses a museum of Swiss history.

•The Fondation Beyeler in Basel, which has a collection of modern and contemporary art.

- The Olympic Museum in Lausanne, which is dedicated to the history of the Olympic Games.

- The Museum of Fine Arts in Geneva, which has a collection of European art from the 14th to the 20th centuries.

- The Paul Klee Center in Bern, which has a collection of works by the artist Paul Klee, as well as other modern and contemporary art.

- The Museum Tinguely in Basel, which is dedicated to the work of the Swiss artist Jean Tinguely.

- The Museum of Communication in Bern, which has a collection of artifacts related to the history of communication, including telegraphs, radios, and telephones.

- The Museum of Natural History in Geneva, which has a collection of specimens and exhibits on the natural world, including fossils, minerals, and live animals.

•The Museum of Transport in Lucerne, which has a collection of vehicles, including cars, trains, and planes, as well as interactive exhibits on transportation history.

•The Jungfraujoch - Top of Europe, which is an interactive museum of the history of the Jungfrau railway and the surrounding area, it's located in the heart of the Swiss Alps.

•The Swiss Museum of Games in La Tour-de-Peilz, which has a collection of games and puzzles from around the world, as well as interactive exhibits on game design and history.

•The Museum of the History of Medicine in Basel, which has a collection of medical instruments, books, and other artifacts from the history of medicine.

- The Museum of Music in Lausanne, which has a collection of instruments, manuscripts, and other artifacts related to the history of music.

- The Museum of Fine Arts in La Chaux-de-Fonds, which has a collection of art from the 19th and 20th centuries, with a focus on the work of local artists.

- The Museum of Art and History in Geneva, which has a collection of art and artifacts from the history of Geneva and the surrounding region.

- The Landesmuseum Zürich, which is the largest cultural and historical museum in Switzerland, with exhibits on Swiss history, art, and culture.

These are some of the top museums in Switzerland, each one of them has a unique collection and offers a different experience.

They are all worth visiting if you have the opportunity.

BEST CHURCHES IN SWITZERLAND
Switzerland is home to many beautiful churches, each with its own unique history and architecture. Some of the most notable include:

•The Cathedral of St. Peter and Paul in Geneva: This Gothic-style cathedral is one of the most important religious sites in Geneva and is known for its stunning stained-glass windows and impressive bell tower.

•The Munster Cathedral in Berne: This Gothic-style cathedral is the oldest church in Berne and is known for its impressive stained-glass windows, intricate carvings, and beautiful frescoes.

•The Church of St. Leodegar in Lucerne: This Baroque-style church is known for its ornate decor and beautiful frescoes and is considered one of the most beautiful churches in Lucerne.

- The Basilica of St. Ursus in Solothurn: This Baroque-style church is the largest in Solothurn and is known for its ornate decor, frescoes and the beautiful organ.

- The Church of St. Martin in Zürich: This medieval-style church is one of the oldest in Zürich and is known for its intricate frescoes and beautiful stained-glass windows.

These are just a few of the many beautiful churches that can be found in Switzerland. Each one offers a unique glimpse into the country's rich religious and cultural history.

BEST PARKS AND GARDENS IN SWITZERLAND

Switzerland is a country known for its stunning natural beauty and breathtaking landscapes, and this extends to its parks and gardens as well. From vibrant gardens filled with blooming flowers to spacious parks offering breathtaking views, Switzerland has something to offer everyone. Here are some of the best parks and gardens in Switzerland that are worth visiting:

•The Rhine Falls Park
Located in the heart of Schaffhausen, the Rhine Falls Park is one of the largest waterfalls in Europe and one of the most popular tourist attractions in Switzerland. The park offers stunning views of the falls and is a popular spot for picnics, walks and other outdoor activities. Visitors can take a boat tour to the falls, walk along the trails, or relax on one of the benches and enjoy the natural beauty.

•The English Garden
The English Garden in Montreux is one of the most beautiful parks in Switzerland and is known for its vibrant flowers, rolling hills, and breathtaking views of Lake Geneva. The park is home to over 300 species of plants

and flowers, making it a popular destination for nature lovers and botanists. Visitors can enjoy a picnic, take a walk along the trails, or simply sit back and relax among the beautiful flowers and greenery.

- The Botanical Garden of the University of Geneva

The Botanical Garden of the University of Geneva is one of the oldest and most respected botanical gardens in Switzerland. It covers over 10 hectares and is home to over 15,000 plant species from all over the world. The garden is divided into several sections, including a Mediterranean garden, a rock garden, and a tropical greenhouse. Visitors can take a guided tour of the garden, attend a lecture, or simply enjoy the peaceful atmosphere and beautiful scenery.

- The Park at the Castle of Gruyères

The Park at the Castle of Gruyères is a beautiful park in the heart of the Swiss Alps. It offers breathtaking views of the surrounding mountains and is a popular spot for picnics, walks, and other outdoor activities. The park is home to several species of birds and animals, including deer and foxes, and visitors can also see the castle ruins from the park.

•The Wasserturm Park
The Wasserturm Park is a beautiful park located in the heart of Zurich. It is one of the largest parks in the city and is known for its stunning views of the city and the surrounding mountains. The park is a popular spot for picnics, walks, and other outdoor activities and is also home to several restaurants and cafes. Visitors can enjoy a relaxing stroll along the trails, take a boat tour of the lake, or simply relax on one of the benches and enjoy the natural beauty.

•The Park at the St. Jakob-Stadium
The Park at the St. Jakob-Stadium is a beautiful park located in the heart of Basel. It offers stunning views of the surrounding

mountains and is a popular spot for picnics, walks, and other outdoor activities. The park is home to several species of birds and animals and visitors can also see the stadium from the park.

•The Flower Garden at the Lake of Thun
The Flower Garden at the Lake of Thun is a beautiful garden located in the heart of Thun. It is one of the largest flower gardens in Switzerland and is known for its vibrant flowers, rolling hills, and breathtaking views of the lake. The garden is home to over 200 species of plants and flowers and visitors can enjoy a picnic, take a walk along the trails, or simply sit back and relax among the beautiful flowers and greenery.

•The Japanese Garden
The Japanese Garden in Zurich is a peaceful oasis in the heart of the city. It is one of the largest Japanese gardens in Europe and is known for its traditional design, tranquil atmosphere, and beautiful scenery. The

garden covers over 7 hectares and is home to several traditional Japanese buildings, including a tea house, a Zen garden, and a pagoda. Visitors can take a guided tour of the garden, attend a meditation or yoga class, or simply relax and soak up the peaceful atmosphere.

•The Park of Nations
The Park of Nations is a beautiful park located in Geneva. It covers over 20 hectares and is home to several species of birds and animals, including deer and foxes. The park is known for its stunning views of the city and the surrounding mountains and is a popular spot for picnics, walks, and other outdoor activities. Visitors can take a boat tour of the lake, enjoy a picnic, or simply relax on one of the benches and enjoy the natural beauty.

•The Rose Garden in Sion
The Rose Garden in Sion is a beautiful garden located in the heart of the Swiss

Alps. It is known for its vibrant roses and breathtaking views of the surrounding mountains. The garden is home to over 1,500 species of roses and is a popular destination for nature lovers and botanists. Visitors can take a guided tour of the garden, attend a lecture, or simply enjoy the peaceful atmosphere and beautiful scenery.

These are just a few of the many beautiful parks and gardens in Switzerland. Whether you are looking for a peaceful escape from the city or a chance to connect with nature, Switzerland has something to offer everyone. So why not take a stroll in one of these breathtaking parks and gardens and soak up the beauty and serenity of this incredible country.

ART GALLERIES IN SWITZERLAND

Switzerland is known for its rich cultural heritage, and this extends to its art galleries as well. From contemporary art exhibitions to classic masterpieces, Switzerland has something to offer everyone. Here are some of the best art galleries in Switzerland that are worth visiting:

•Kunstmuseum Bern
The Kunstmuseum Bern is one of the largest art museums in Switzerland and is located in the heart of the city of Bern. The museum is home to over 4,000 works of art, including paintings, sculptures, and drawings, dating from the 15th century to the present day. Visitors can admire works by Swiss and international artists, including Pablo Picasso, Paul Klee, and Alberto Giacometti, among others.

•The Museum of Fine Arts (MFA) in Lausanne
The Museum of Fine Arts in Lausanne is one of the largest art museums in Switzerland and is home to over 100,000 works of art, including paintings, sculptures, and drawings, dating from the Middle Ages to the present day. Visitors can admire works

by Swiss and international artists, including Fragonard, Botticelli, and Cézanne, among others.

•The Art Museum Winterthur
The Art Museum Winterthur is a beautiful museum located in the heart of Winterthur. The museum is home to over 90,000 works of art, including paintings, sculptures, and drawings, dating from the Middle Ages to the present day. Visitors can admire works by Swiss and international artists, including Rembrandt, Gainsborough, and Monet, among others.

•The Museum of Art Lucerne (Kunstmuseum Luzern)
The Museum of Art Lucerne is a beautiful museum located in the heart of Lucerne. The museum is home to over 3,000 works of art, including paintings, sculptures, and drawings, dating from the Middle Ages to the present day. Visitors can admire works

by Swiss and international artists, including Dürer, Vermeer, and Monet, among others.

•The Museum of Art and History (MAH) in Geneva
The Museum of Art and History in Geneva is one of the largest art museums in Switzerland and is home to over 2,000 works of art, including paintings, sculptures, and drawings, dating from the Middle Ages to the present day. Visitors can admire works by Swiss and international artists, including Rubens, Renoir, and Cézanne, among others.

•The Fondation de l'Hermitage in Lausanne
The Fondation de l'Hermitage in Lausanne is a beautiful museum located in the heart of Lausanne. The museum is home to over 3,000 works of art, including paintings, sculptures, and drawings, dating from the Middle Ages to the present day. Visitors can admire works by Swiss and international

artists, including Cézanne, Renoir, and Monet, among others.

•The Museum of Art Thun (Kunstmuseum Thun)
The Museum of Art Thun is a beautiful museum located in the heart of Thun. The museum is home to over 2,000 works of art, including paintings, sculptures, and drawings, dating from the Middle Ages to the present day. Visitors can admire works by Swiss and international artists, including Rembrandt, Vermeer, and Monet, among others.

•The Museum Rietberg in Zurich
The Museum Rietberg in Zurich is a beautiful museum located in the heart of Zurich. The museum is home to over 30,000 works of art, including paintings,sculptures, and drawings, from Asia, Africa, America, and Oceania. Visitors can admire works by indigenous artists, including African masks, Japanese ukiyo-e prints, and ancient

Chinese pottery, among others. The museum also offers various exhibitions and cultural events, such as dance performances, film screenings, and workshops.

•The Museum of Design in Zurich (Museum für Gestaltung)
The Museum of Design in Zurich is one of the largest design museums in Switzerland and is located in the heart of Zurich. The museum is home to over 500,000 works of design, including graphic design, product design, and fashion design, from the 19th century to the present day. Visitors can admire works by Swiss and international designers, including Le Corbusier, Charles and Ray Eames, and Alexander McQueen, among others.

•The Museum of Ethnography in Geneva (Musée d'ethnographie de Genève)
The Museum of Ethnography in Geneva is a beautiful museum located in the heart of Geneva. The museum is home to over

250,000 works of ethnography, including textiles, ceramics, and sculptures, from various cultures around the world. Visitors can admire works by indigenous artists, including African masks, South American textiles, and Native American pottery, among others. The museum also offers various exhibitions and cultural events, such as dance performances, film screenings, and workshops.

These are just a few of the many art galleries in Switzerland that are worth visiting. Whether you are an art enthusiast, a design lover, or simply interested in exploring different cultures, Switzerland has something to offer everyone. So why not visit one of these incredible museums and experience the beauty and diversity of Swiss art and culture.

CHAPTER TWO

TRAVEL SMART
THINGS TO KNOW BEFORE VISITING SWITZERLAND

Here is a concise summary of things to know before visiting Switzerland:

•Geography: Switzerland is located in Central Europe, surrounded by France, Italy, Austria, and Germany. The country is known for its natural beauty, including the Swiss Alps, lakes, and scenic train routes.

•Language: Swiss German, French, Italian, and Romansh are the official languages of Switzerland. English is widely spoken, particularly in tourist areas.

•Currency: Swiss Franc (CHF) is the currency used in Switzerland. Most places accept credit and debit cards, but it's always a good idea to carry some cash.

- Transportation: Switzerland has an excellent public transportation system, including trains, buses, and trams. A Swiss Travel Pass is a convenient option for visiting multiple destinations.

- Accommodation: Switzerland offers a wide range of accommodations, from budget-friendly hostels to luxury hotels. Booking in advance is recommended, especially during peak tourist season.

- Food: Swiss cuisine is influenced by French, German, and Italian cooking styles. Cheese and chocolate are two of the country's specialties. Fondue, a dish made of melted cheese and bread, is a popular option.

- Activities: Switzerland offers a variety of outdoor activities, including skiing, snowboarding, hiking, and mountain biking. Urban areas like Zurich and Geneva offer cultural attractions, shopping, and dining.

- Safety: Switzerland is known for its low crime rate and safety. However, it's still a good idea to take standard safety precautions, such as being aware of your surroundings and avoiding carrying large amounts of cash.

- Visa Requirements: Switzerland is part of the Schengen Area, and visitors from certain countries may need a visa to enter. Check the visa requirements for your country before traveling.

- Tipping: Tipping is not mandatory in Switzerland, but it's common to leave a small amount for good service in restaurants and taxis.

This should provide you with a good overview of things to know before visiting Switzerland. I hope you have a great trip!

GETTING HERE AND AROUND IN SWITZERLAND

As a highly developed and modern country, Switzerland boasts an efficient and well-connected transportation system.

Switzerland's public transportation network includes trains, buses, and trams, all of which are operated by the Swiss Federal Railways. The trains are the most popular mode of transportation and are known for their punctuality and cleanliness. They connect major cities and towns, and many of them offer scenic views of the Swiss Alps.

In addition to trains, Switzerland also has an extensive network of buses and trams that serve smaller towns and villages. They are often used by commuters to get to and from work and are also popular with tourists.

Switzerland's airports are also well-connected and offer flights to cities around the world. The main airport, Zurich Airport, is one of the busiest in Europe and serves as a hub for Swiss International Air Lines.

Driving in Switzerland is relatively easy, with well-maintained roads and highways. However, due to the mountainous terrain, some roads can be narrow and winding, and there are strict traffic regulations that must be followed.

Overall, Switzerland's transportation system is reliable, efficient, and convenient, making it easy for tourists and locals to explore the country and get from one place to another.

ESSENTIALS
•Passport/ID: Swiss immigration requires a valid passport or national ID card.

•Cash/Cards: Swiss francs or a debit/credit card to access ATMs and make purchases.

- Clothing: Warm and waterproof clothing, especially for winter or alpine activities.

- Insurance: Travel insurance for medical, trip cancellations, and emergency situations.

- Adaptors: Swiss electrical outlets use type C and J plugs, so consider bringing a plug adaptor.

- Map/Guidebook: To navigate and plan your trip, especially for scenic destinations.

- Camera: To capture stunning memories of Swiss landscapes, architecture, and culture.

- Water bottle: To stay hydrated and reduce plastic waste.

- Medications: Any prescription medications and first-aid supplies, as well as insect repellent for summer trips.

- Transportation: Consider purchasing a Swiss Travel Pass for unlimited public transportation, or rent a car for exploring the countryside.

- Comfortable shoes: For walking and hiking, especially for mountainous terrain.

- Luggage lock: To secure your belongings in shared accommodations or during transit.

- Sunscreen: For protection from the sun, especially for outdoor activities.

- Language phrasebook: Swiss languages include German, French, Italian, and Romansh, so it helps to have a basic knowledge of at least one.

- Local cuisine: Try the famous Swiss cheeses, chocolate, and Raclette while in Switzerland.

- Entertainment: Books, games, or a tablet for entertainment during downtime or travel.

- Umbrella: For sudden rain showers, especially in spring or autumn.

- ID copies: Photocopies of passport or ID card, as well as insurance policy and emergency contact information.

- Portable charger: To keep devices charged while on the go.

- Winter gear: If visiting in winter, bring appropriate gear such as gloves, hats, and thermal underwear.

WHAT TO WEAR FOR EVERY SEASON IN SWITZERLAND
Spring (March-May)

During the spring season, the weather in Switzerland can be quite unpredictable and can vary from cool and rainy to warm and sunny. It is best to pack light layers such as a long-sleeved shirt, a light jacket, and a waterproof raincoat. A hat and comfortable shoes are also essential for exploring the countryside during this time of year.

Summer (June-August)

Summer in Switzerland is usually warm and sunny, with temperatures ranging from 20-30°C. Light, breathable clothing such as cotton t-shirts, shorts, and skirts are ideal for the warm weather. Sunscreen and sunglasses are also essential to protect your skin from the sun. It's also a good idea to pack a lightweight sweater or jacket in case the weather turns cool in the evenings.

Fall (September-November)

Fall in Switzerland is characterized by cool, crisp weather, with temperatures ranging from 10-20°C. It is important to pack layers such as a sweater, a jacket, and a scarf to keep warm during this time of year. A waterproof jacket is also essential in case of rain. Comfortable shoes are important for exploring the countryside during this time of year.

Winter (December-February)

Winter in Switzerland can be very cold, with temperatures often dropping below freezing. It is important to pack warm clothing such as a heavy jacket, a hat, gloves, and a scarf to keep warm during this time of year. Snow boots or waterproof boots are also essential for navigating the snow and ice.

In conclusion, the key to dressing for the seasons in Switzerland is to pack layers and be prepared for changing weather conditions. Whether you're visiting during the summer or winter, it's always a good idea to have a waterproof jacket and comfortable shoes.

HELPFUL SWISS PHRASES

Here are some useful Swiss German phrases and their pronunciation:

- Hallo (hah-loh) - Hello
- Guten Morgen (goo-ten mawr-gen) - Good morning
- Wie geht es Ihnen? (vee gayt es ee-nen) - How are you?
- Mir geht es gut, danke. (meer gayt es goot, dahn-keh) - I'm fine, thank you.
- Entschuldigung (en-shool-dee-goong) - Excuse me
- Bitte (bit-teh) - Please
- Danke (dahn-keh) - Thank you
- Ja (yah) - Yes
- Nein (nine) - No
- Ich heisse ... (ihk heiss-eh) - My name is...
- Wo ist ...? (voh ist ...?) - Where is ...?
- Ich suche ... (ihk zoosh-eh) - I'm looking for ...
- Ich verstehe nicht (ihk fehr-shtay-eh nihcht) - I don't understand

- Können Sie mir helfen? (kern-en zee meer hel-fen?) - Can you help me?
- Ich spreche kein Deutsch (ihk shpreh-eh kine doytsh) - I don't speak German
- Ich möchte ... (ihk merk-teh) - I would like ...
- Wie viel kostet es? (vee-viel kos-tet es?) - How much does it cost?
- Ich bin müde (ihk bin mue-deh) - I'm tired
- Ich bin hungrig (ihk bin hoong-rik) - I'm hungry
- Ich habe Durst (ihk hah-beh doorst) - I'm thirsty.

GREAT ITINERARIES

Switzerland offers a wealth of diverse experiences for travelers, from scenic alpine landscapes and quaint villages to bustling cities and rich cultural heritage. Here are a few popular itinerary options for exploring this beautiful country:

- Swiss Alps Adventure: A great itinerary for adventure-seekers, this tour takes you to the iconic mountain resorts of Zermatt, Grindelwald, and Lucerne, where you can go skiing, snowboarding, ice skating, and more. Visit the Matterhorn, Europe's most recognizable mountain peak, and take a scenic train journey through the Swiss Alps.

•Lake Geneva & the Swiss Riviera: For those who love stunning natural beauty and tranquil lakeside towns, this itinerary takes you to the stunning Lake Geneva region, where you can visit the elegant cities of Geneva, Montreux, Lausanne, and Vevey. Enjoy scenic boat rides, explore local vineyards, and stroll along the shores of Lake Geneva.

•Swiss Mountain Experience: This itinerary takes you to Interlaken, the heart of the Swiss Alps, where you can explore the stunning Lauterbrunnen Valley and take the Mount Pilatus cable car for panoramic views of the surrounding peaks. Take a scenic train journey and enjoy outdoor activities such as hiking and mountain biking.

- Swiss City Tour: For those interested in Swiss history and culture, this itinerary takes you to the cities of Zurich, Bern, and Lucerne, where you can visit museums, historical landmarks, and local markets. Stroll along the picturesque Old Town areas and enjoy a scenic boat ride on Lake Zurich.

- Swiss Culture & History: This itinerary takes you to St. Moritz, Chur, and Appenzell, where you can learn about Switzerland's rich cultural heritage, including traditional crafts, folk music, and local customs. Explore charming villages and scenic mountain landscapes, and visit local museums and historical sites.

- Swiss Scenic Rail: For those who love scenic train journeys, this itinerary takes you from Zermatt to St. Moritz on the Glacier Express, one of the most scenic rail journeys in the world. Admire breathtaking mountain scenery, crystal-clear lakes, and picturesque villages along the way.

•Swiss Christmas Market Tour: For those looking to experience a traditional Swiss Christmas, this itinerary takes you to Zurich, Lucerne, and Montreux to visit local Christmas markets and enjoy festive events. Take scenic train rides, explore local landmarks, and enjoy the cozy atmosphere of the holiday season.

•Swiss Chocolate & Cheese Indulgence: For those with a sweet tooth, this itinerary takes you to Gruyères, Lucerne, and Zurich, where you can indulge in local specialties such as Swiss chocolate and cheese. Visit local chocolate factories, cheese dairies, and enjoy scenic walks in the countryside.

•Swiss Wildlife & Nature: This itinerary takes you to Interlaken and the Lauterbrunnen Valley, where you can admire breathtaking natural beauty and spot local wildlife such as ibex, chamois, and marmots. Take scenic walks and enjoy outdoor activities such as hiking and kayaking.

•Swiss Art & Architecture: This itinerary takes you to the cities of Basel, Lausanne, and Geneva, where you can admire world-class art and architecture, including modernist buildings and contemporary art galleries. Visit local museums, art exhibitions, and historic landmarks, and enjoy scenic boat rides on Lake Geneva.

CHAPTER THREE

ACCOMMODATIONS
BEST PLACE TO EAT, SLEEP AND RELAX

Here's a brief overview of the best places to eat, sleep, and relax in Switzerland.

-Eating: Switzerland has a rich culinary tradition that showcases the country's diverse geography, history, and culture. From traditional Swiss dishes like raclette and fondue to international cuisine, Switzerland has something for every taste. Here are a few of the best places to eat in Switzerland:

•La table d'Edgard in Lausanne: This contemporary Swiss restaurant offers an innovative and diverse menu that features seasonal ingredients and classic Swiss dishes with a modern twist. The restaurant is known for its warm ambiance and exceptional service, making it the perfect place for a special night out.

•St. Gallerhof in St. Gallen: This traditional Swiss restaurant serves classic Swiss dishes made with the freshest ingredients. The menu includes hearty dishes like rösti (a Swiss potato dish) and a variety of cheese-based dishes like fondue and raclette. The restaurant is known for its warm and welcoming atmosphere, making it the perfect place to enjoy a delicious meal with friends and family.

•Gasthaus zur Linde in Lucerne: This charming restaurant offers fresh Swiss specialties made with locally sourced ingredients. The menu includes classic Swiss dishes like veal cordon bleu and roasted meats, as well as vegetarian options. The restaurant is known for its cozy atmosphere and friendly service, making it the perfect place to relax and enjoy a delicious meal.

-Sleeping: Switzerland offers a wide range of accommodation options, from luxury hotels to cozy bed and breakfasts. Here are a few of the best places to stay in Switzerland:

•Grand Hotel Quellenhof in Bad Ragaz: This luxury hotel is located in the heart of the Swiss Alps and offers breathtaking views of the surrounding mountains. The hotel features a variety of room options, including spacious suites with private balconies and fireplaces. The hotel also features a world-class spa and wellness center, making it the perfect place to relax and rejuvenate.

•Hotel Alexander in Zermatt: This charming hotel is located in the heart of the Swiss Alps and offers stunning views of the Matterhorn. The hotel features a variety of room options, including cozy rooms with traditional Swiss decor and spacious suites with private balconies. The hotel is known for its warm and welcoming atmosphere, making it the perfect place to unwind after a day of exploring.

•Hotel Waldhaus Sils in Engadin: This peaceful hotel is located in the heart of the Swiss Alps and offers breathtaking views of the surrounding mountains. The hotel features a variety of room options, including cozy rooms with traditional Swiss decor and spacious suites with private balconies. The hotel is known for its tranquil atmosphere and exceptional service, making it the perfect place to relax and recharge.

-Relaxing: Switzerland is known for its stunning natural beauty and tranquil atmosphere, making it the perfect place to relax and unwind. Here are a few of the best places to relax in Switzerland:

•Therme Vals in Vals: This thermal bath complex offers a variety of indoor and outdoor pools, as well as saunas and steam rooms. The complex is located in the heart of the Swiss Alps and offers breathtaking views of the surrounding mountains.

•Wellness Resort Les Bains d'Ovronnaz in Ovronnaz: This spa and wellness resort offers a variety of treatments, including massage therapy, hydrotherapy, and beauty treatments. The resort is located in the heart of the Swiss Alps and offers breathtaking views of the surrounding mountains. The resort is known for its warm and welcoming atmosphere and exceptional service, making it the perfect place to relax and rejuvenate.

•Lake Geneva: This stunning lake is located in the heart of Switzerland and offers scenic walks, boating, and a variety of water sports. The lake is surrounded by charming towns and villages, making it the perfect place to explore and relax. The lake is also home to several parks and gardens, making it the perfect place to spend a day surrounded by nature.

In conclusion, Switzerland offers a wealth of options for dining, sleeping, and relaxing, making it a perfect destination for travelers of all interests and budgets. Whether you are looking for a luxurious spa retreat, a cozy bed and breakfast, or a traditional Swiss restaurant, Switzerland has something for everyone.

ENTERTAINMENT AND NIGHTLIFE

Switzerland is a country known for its stunning natural scenery, rich cultural heritage, and modern lifestyle. It is also known for its nightlife and entertainment options that cater to a wide range of interests and tastes. The country is renowned for its vibrant nightlife and entertainment scene that offers a range of activities and events to keep visitors entertained throughout the night. From live music performances, cultural events, nightclubs, and bars, Switzerland is a country that truly never sleeps.

Music is an integral part of Switzerland's nightlife and entertainment scene, and the country is home to a number of music festivals and events that draw visitors from all over the world. The renowned Montreux Jazz Festival, for example, is one of the largest and oldest jazz festivals in the world and has been running since 1967. The festival is held annually in July and attracts a wide range of local and international musicians and music lovers.

Another popular music festival in Switzerland is the Paleo Festival Nyon, which is held annually in the town of Nyon and features a range of musical genres including rock, pop, and electronic music. The festival is known for its eclectic line-up and attracts a large number of visitors each year.

For those looking for a more laid-back entertainment experience, Switzerland's many theaters, cinemas, and opera houses provide a range of cultural events that cater to a variety of tastes. The Theater 11 in Zurich, for example, is a popular destination for those interested in contemporary theater and dance performances.

Nightclubs and bars are also a major part of Switzerland's nightlife and entertainment scene, with a wide range of options available for those looking to dance the night away. Some of the most popular nightclubs in Switzerland include the Plaza Club in Zurich, the D! Club in Lausanne, and the Hive Club in Zurich. These nightclubs offer a range of music styles including electronic, hip-hop, and rock, and are popular with both locals and visitors alike.

In addition to nightclubs, Switzerland is home to a number of bars that cater to a variety of tastes and interests. The Long Street Café in Zurich, for example, is a popular destination for those interested in craft beers, while the Bar Rouge in Geneva is a popular spot for those looking for a chic and trendy bar experience.

For those looking for a more relaxed and intimate entertainment experience, Switzerland's many wine bars and lounges are the perfect option. These bars are known for their high-quality wine selections, and many also offer a range of small plates and light bites to accompany the wine. Some of the most popular wine bars in Switzerland include the Wine Bar in Zurich, the Wine Lounge in Geneva, and the Wine Room in Lausanne.

In addition to its nightlife and entertainment options, Switzerland is also known for its cultural events and activities, which provide a range of activities for visitors to enjoy. From museums and galleries to festivals and fairs, Switzerland's cultural scene is vibrant and diverse, and offers a range of events and activities for visitors to enjoy.

The Art Basel fair, for example, is one of the largest and most prestigious art fairs in the world and is held annually in Basel. The fair attracts a large number of visitors each year, including art lovers, collectors, and curators, and features a wide range of modern and contemporary artworks from leading international artists.

Another popular cultural event in Switzerland is the International Film Festival in Locarno, which is held annually in August and attracts a large number of visitors each year. The festival showcases a range of films from both established and emerging filmmakers, and is a popular destination for those interested in the latest trends in international cinema.

For those interested in Switzerland's rich cultural heritage, the country is home to a number of museums and galleries that showcase its rich history and artistic heritage. The Swiss National Museum in Zurich, for example, is a popular destination for those interested in Swiss history, while the Kunsthaus in Zurich showcases a range of contemporary and modern artworks.

In addition to its museums and galleries, Switzerland is also known for its festivals and fairs, which provide a range of activities and events for visitors to enjoy. The Geneva International Film Festival, for example, is held annually in November and features a range of films from both established and emerging filmmakers. The festival is a popular destination for those interested in the latest trends in international cinema.

For those interested in outdoor activities, Switzerland offers a range of options for visitors to enjoy. From hiking and skiing to water sports and climbing, the country's stunning natural scenery provides a range of activities for visitors to enjoy. The Swiss Alps, for example, are a popular destination for those interested in skiing and snowboarding, while Lake Geneva is a popular destination for those interested in water sports and boating.

In conclusion, Switzerland is a country that offers a range of nightlife and entertainment options to cater to a wide range of interests and tastes. From live music performances, cultural events, nightclubs, and bars to festivals, fairs, and outdoor activities, Switzerland is a country that truly never sleeps and offers a range of activities for visitors to enjoy. Whether you are interested in the latest trends in international cinema, contemporary art, or outdoor activities, Switzerland is a destination that is sure to provide a memorable and enjoyable experience for all.

CHAPTER FOUR

FUN FACTS ABOUT SWITZERLAND
•Switzerland is known for its neutral stance, and has not participated in a war since 1815.

•Swiss chocolate is considered some of the best in the world and is renowned for its high quality and rich flavor.

•The Swiss are famous for their precision and efficiency, and Swiss trains are renowned for their punctuality and cleanliness.

•Switzerland has four official languages: German, French, Italian, and Romansh.

•Switzerland is the birthplace of the Red Cross, which was founded in 1863 by Swiss businessman Henry Dunant.

•The Swiss Army Knife is a popular and iconic tool that is used by people all over the world.

•Switzerland is home to several famous and prestigious universities, including the University of Geneva and the University of Zurich.

•Switzerland is known for its stunning natural scenery, including the Swiss Alps, Lake Geneva, and the Rhine Falls.

- The Swiss banking industry is one of the most highly developed and respected in the world, and Switzerland is home to several of the world's largest banks.

- Switzerland is a popular destination for skiing and snowboarding, and is home to several world-renowned ski resorts, including Verbier, Zermatt, and St. Moritz.

- The Swiss Flag is a red square with a white cross in the center, and is considered one of the simplest and most recognizable flags in the world.

- The Swiss economy is considered one of the strongest and most stable in the world, and Switzerland has a high standard of living and low unemployment rate.

- The Swiss are known for their love of chocolate, cheese, and wine, and these products are a major part of the country's cuisine and culture.

- Switzerland is home to several famous and historic watch brands, including Omega, Rolex, and Patek Philippe.

- The Matterhorn is a famous mountain located in the Swiss Alps and is one of the most recognizable landmarks in the world.

- Switzerland is famous for its cheese, with over 450 different varieties produced in the country, including Gruyere, Emmental, and Raclette.

- The Swiss Federal Constitution is one of the oldest constitutions in the world and has been in force since 1848.

- Switzerland is a popular destination for tourists and is known for its stunning natural scenery, rich cultural heritage, and modern lifestyle.

•The Swiss Franc is the official currency of Switzerland and is considered one of the strongest and most stable currencies in the world.

•Switzerland is a member of the United Nations and is home to several international organizations, including the World Trade Organization and the World Health Organization.

Printed in the USA
CPSIA information can be obtained
at www.ICGtesting.com
LVHW012039250823
756246LV00028B/391